Mysteries Of The Bible
Volume I

Mysteries Of The Bible
Volume I

Written By:

Pastor Ulysses L. Norris

Edited By: Alitra Wynn and Alison Norris

Copyright © 2009 by Pastor Ulysses L. Norris.

ISBN: Hardcover   978-1-4415-0506-4
           Softcover   978-1-4415-0505-7

All rights reserved. No part of this book may be reproduced or transmitted in any form or by any means, electronic or mechanical, including photocopying, recording, or by any information storage and retrieval system, without permission in writing from the copyright owner.

This book was printed in the United States of America.

To order additional copies of this book, contact:
Xlibris Corporation
1-888-795-4274
www.Xlibris.com
Orders@Xlibris.com
56307

Contents

Foreword ix

Mysteries Of The Bible—Volume I 1

Mystery Of The Coat Of Many Colours 7

The Mystery Of Who Will Be Given Knowledge 10

Mystery Of The Sons Of God 20

The Dream Of The Terrible Image 26

The Vision Of The Seventy Weeks 33

God's And Satan's Conversation About Job 42

The Mystery Of The Olive Trees 46

The Mystery Of The New Jerusalem 50

The Mystery Of The Victory Over Death 55

Prayer 69

To God be the glory, honor, and the praise. Thanks be to the only wise God who gives wisdom and knowledge.

I DEDICATE THIS BOOK TO MY FATHER IN THE GOSPEL AND MENTOR, BISHOP WILLIAM L. BONNER WHOSE INSPIRATIONAL LEADERSHIP HAS ALREADY PRODUCED FRUIT A HUNDRED FOLD. HE HAS DEDICATED MOST OF HIS LIFE TO THE SERVICE OF OUR LORD AND SAVIOR JESUS CHRIST, TO BE A BLESSING TO MILLIONS OF LOST SOULS. HE HAS ADDED TO THE NUMBER OF SOULS THE TRUTH OF GOD'S WORD. HE HAS BEEN USED BY GOD TO LEAD MANY TO THE LIGHT OF THE TRUTH IN GOD'S WORD.

I ALSO DEDICATE THIS BOOK TO ALL THE PASTORS AND CHILDREN OF GOD, TO ENCOURAGE YOU TO KEEP THE FAITH AND STAND STRONG IN THESE LAST AND EVIL DAYS WHILE YOU JOURNEY THROUGH THIS LIFE. MAY GOD BLESS YOU.

I GIVE THANKS AND GRATITUDE TO MY LOVING WIFE, ALICE NORRIS, WHO HELPED INSPIRE ME TO WRITE THIS BOOK.

Foreword

This book offers the understanding of some of the mysteries in the Bible. It deals with mysteries of God. Paul said in II Corinthians 11:25-27,

> *"Thrice was I beaten with rods, once was I stoned, thrice I suffered shipwreck, a night and a day I have been in the deep; In journeyings often, in perils of waters, in perils of robbers, in perils by mine own countrymen, in perils by the heathen, in perils in the city, in perils in the wilderness, in perils in the sea, in perils among false brethren; In weariness and painfulness, in watchings often, in hunger and thirst, in fastings often, in cold and nakedness."*

Being chosen by God, and going through these things allowed Paul to be able to say,

> *"And though I have the gift of prophecy, and understand all mysteries, and all knowledge; and though I have all faith, so that I could remove mountains, and have not charity, I am nothing."*—I Corinthians 13:2

The most important gift one can receive and share with others is LOVE.

Mysteries Of The Bible
Volume I

I have read the Pre-Adamic man: "Were there human beings on Earth before Adam?" by Russell Grigg, and the teachings of Hugh Ross. I have read of the theory of Frenchman Isaac La Peyrere pre-Adamic stock, written in 1655. I have also read of Darwinism. However, as noted American evangelical theologian Dr. John MacArthur says, "Scripture, not science, is the ultimate of all truth," and that is a fact. These are the facts.

> *"Daniel answered in the presence of the king, and said, The secret which the king hath demanded cannot the wise men, the astrologers, the magicians, the soothsayers, show unto the king: But there is a God in heaven that revealeth secrets, and maketh known to the king Nebuchadnezzar what shall be in the latter days. Thy dream, and the visions of thy head upon thy bed, are these; As for thee, O king, thy thoughts came into thy mind upon thy bed, what should come to pass hereafter: and he that revealeth secrets maketh known to thee what shall come to pass. But as for me, this secret is not revealed to me for any wisdom that I have more than any living, but for their sakes that shall make known the interpretation to the king, and that thou mightest know the thoughts of thy heart."*—Daniel 2:27-30

The Bible is a book that is filled with the revelations of God, not men. It was not created by the mind of mankind, therefore, it can not be read and understood as a novel which is authored by the mind of man. It did not come from carnal minds, it is of God, and God is an omnipotent, omniscient Spiritual entity. These sacred and holy scriptures were all **"given by inspiration of God, and are profitable for doctrine, for reproof, for correction, for instruction in righteousness that the man of God may be perfect thoroughly furnished unto all good works."**

Within the scriptures lie many things that the natural mind can not comprehend for they are spiritual.

> *"For they that are after the flesh do mind the things of the flesh; but they that are after the Spirit the things of the Spirit"*—Romans 8:5

> *"Because the carnal mind is enmity against God: for it is not subject to the law of God, neither indeed can be."*—Romans 8:7

The mysteries of God begin in the first book of the Holy Bible, Genesis chapter one, verse one, God's creation of the world, however, chapter one, verse two states that the creation of God was void. God did not create the world in verse one void, He did not fashion an ineffective, or useless world. A mystery lies between verse one and verse two. The creation in verse one was separate and a part from the creation that took place in verse two.

> ***In the beginning God created the heaven and the earth.***—verse 2—***And the earth was without form, and void; and darkness was upon the face of the deep. And the Spirit of God moved upon the face of the waters.***—Genesis 1:1,2

In verse one, there were created living creatures that were not a part of the creation in verse two. The creatures that were created in verse one are the fossils that archaeologist have excavated over the years. The fossils are of what is called the Mesozoic era of the Geological era, after the Paleozoic, and the Cenozoic era. They are the remains of both the dinosaurs and Neanderthal. These creatures that are being excavated and being studied are of the life and culture of ancient people and beasts whose lives began far before that of Adam and Eve. Scientists believe and feel they have proof that Adam and Eve could not have been the first man and woman that God created and they are right!! Please do not close this book just yet, bear with me for a minute, because that does not prove that the bible is wrong, it proves that the bible is right.

Once again, these people and creatures lived billions of years ago, far before Adam and Eve. They lived during the period when Lucifer command was only eclipsed by God. He tried to take over Heaven and Earth, so God then kicked him and the one third of the angels that followed him out of Heaven.

> *"And his tail drew the third part of the stars of heaven, and did cast them to the earth: and the dragon stood before the woman which was ready to be delivered, for to devour her child as soon as it was born"*—Revelation 12:4

It was then that God destroyed all the people and creatures in verse 1 by flood, causing His creation to be made void. And when God come for His saints at the end of this world as we know it, He is going to create this world form from it's foundation up all over again. God is going to create for <u>His</u> children (the saints) a New Heaven and New Earth because at the time of the end it will be destroyed by fire.

After God had made the world void in Genesis 1:1, it was then in verse two of Genesis that God stepped back out billions of years later and began to create what we know as <u>"OUR BEGINNING"</u>. Everything that God created, He saw that is was <u>good</u>. Then when he got to Genesis 1:20, the creation of living creatures, God saw that it was <u>good</u>. Nothing He created was void; everything that God creates is always <u>good</u>.

Then He gave all the living creatures a charge to be fruitful and multiply. In other words, God told them to fill the world with their kind. When it came to man, he said in Genesis 1:26,

> . . . *"Let <u>us</u> make man in <u>our</u> image, after <u>our</u> likeness:"* . . .

I have heard many schools of thought on who God was talking to when he said *"Let us make man:"* The word of God lets us know that it was the Creator and the Redeemer. In order to be in the image of God and Jesus, we had to be part spirit and part flesh. The word of God lets us know that **"God is a Spirit and they that worship Him, must worship Him in spirit and in truth."** So man had to be part spirit and part flesh. Then in Colossians 1:15, it tells us this about Jesus.

> *"(Who) is the image of the invisible God, the <u>first-born</u> of <u>every creature:</u>"*

No creature came forth before Jesus, he have the preeminence in all things.

> *"And he is before all things, and by him <u>all things</u> consist."*—Colossians 1:17

God created the visible part of man which was the flesh, so man became flesh and spirit, which means that if we are flesh and spirit creatures, then this has to be the image that God wanted to reveal because we were made in His likeness and image.

> *"So God created man in his own image, in the image of God created he him; male and female created he them,"*—Genesis 1:27

Jesus was the first creation of God, before Lucifer, before the angels, before the world. That is why he said in St. Luke 10:18,

> *"And he said unto them, I beheld Satan as lightning fall from heaven."*

In other words, Jesus was saying, I saw Satan falling when he was kicked out of Heaven; I was there before Mary brought me forth as a baby boy. I even came in another name and as another man, but the same body. His name was Melchisedec, King of Salem.

> *"And Melchisedec king of Salem brought forth bread and wine: and he was the priest of the most high God."*—Genesis 14:18

> *"The Lord hath sworn, and will not repent, Thou art a priest for ever after the order of Melchisedec."*—Psalm 110:4

> *"So also Christ glorified not himself to be made an high priest; but he that said unto him, Thou art my Son, today I have begotten thee As he saith also in another place, Thou art a priest for ever after the order of Melchisedec. Who*

in the days of his flesh, when he had offered up prayers and supplications with strong crying and tears unto him that was able to save him from death, and was heard in that he feared; Though he were a Son, yet learned he obedience by the things which he suffered. And being made perfect, he became the author of eternal salvation unto all them that obey him; Called of God an high priest after the order of Melchisedec. Of whom we have many things to say, and hard to be uttered, seeing ye are dull of hearing. For when for the time ye ought to be teachers, ye have need that one teach you again which be the first principles of the oracles of God; and are become such as have need of milk, and not of strong meat. For every one that useth milk is unskilful in the word of righteousness: for he is a babe"—Hebrews 5:5-13

"For this Melchisedec, king of Salem, priest of the most high God, who met Abraham returning from the slaughter of the kings, and blessed him; To whom also Abraham gave a tenth part of all; first being by interpretation King of righteousness, and after that also King of Salem, which is, King of peace; Without father, without mother, without descent, having neither beginning of days, nor end of life; but made like unto the Son of God; abideth a priest continually. Now consider how great this man was, unto whom even the patriarch Abraham gave the tenth of the spoils. And verily they that are of the sons of Levi, who receive the office of the priesthood, have a commandment to take tithes of the people according to the law, that is, of their brethren, though they come out of the loins of Abraham:"—Hebrews 7:1-5

Then God gave Adam and Eve a different charge than all the other creatures. He told them to be fruitful and multiply, but then he said something different. He told Adam and Eve to redo something that had already been done before them. He said to <u>replenish</u> the earth. It was the very same charge he gave to Noah and his three sons, Ham, Shem, and Japheth, after He had again destroyed the world by water. He said in Genesis 9:1,

. . . "Be fruitful, and multiply, and <u>replenish</u> the earth." . . .

God wanted mankind and beasts to grow to great numbers. Every living creature except man was new in this world that we live in today. The only creatures that lived before were man and woman, they only looked different. Satan knew who was the weaker vessel from the world before the flood that you read about in Genesis 1:1, so he knew exactly who to come after.

Mystery Of The Coat Of Many Colours

"Now Israel loved Joseph more than all his children, because he was the son of his old age: and he made him a coat of many colours."—Genesis 37:3

Joseph was 17, a young man who loved God, and loved his brothers so much that he was determined to bless them by doing something that would help them. Sometimes, trying to help someone can cause you to be alienated, and cause some people to hate you because of your right decisions. So he told his father of their evil reports and his father, who loved him, made him a coat of many colors. This coat represented every creed, color, and nationality, of all people of the world. Abraham passed on to his son Joseph, the blessings promised to him.

"Now the Lord had said unto Abram, Get thee out of thy country, and from thy kindred, and from thy father's house, unto a land that I will show thee: And I will make of thee a great nation, and I will bless thee, and make thy name great; and thou shalt be a blessing: And I will bless them that bless thee, and curse him that curseth thee: and in thee shall all families of the earth be blessed."—Genesis 12:1-3

Then came the dreams, which caused his brothers to hate him even more. They did not understand that everything that was taking place was of God. If you are chosen by God to do His will, your steps are ordered by Him. Joseph's first dream from God was this.

> *"And Joseph dreamed a dream, and he told it his brethren: and they hated him yet the more. And he said unto them, Hear, I pray you, this dream which I have dreamed: For, behold, we were binding sheaves in the field, and, lo, my sheaf arose, and also stood upright; and, behold, your sheaves stood round about, and made obeisance to my sheaf. And his brethren said to him, Shalt thou indeed reign over us? or shalt thou indeed have dominion over us? And they hated him yet the more for his dreams, and for his words."*—Genesis 37:5-8

God was revealing to Joseph's brothers that he was going to reign over them, and that he would have dominion over them. Then in Genesis 37:9-11, Joseph had a second dream from God that was a mystery.

> *"And he dreamed yet another dream, and told it his brethren, and said, Behold, I have dreamed a dream more; and, behold, the sun and the moon and the eleven stars made obeisance to me. And he told it to his father, and to his brethren: and his father rebuked him, and said unto him, What is this dream that thou hast dreamed? Shall I and thy mother and thy brethren indeed come to bow down ourselves to thee to the earth? And his brethren envied him; but his father observed the saying."*

This dream that was revealed to Joseph was a dream about a sun, moon and eleven stars that bowed down to him. God was revealing to Joseph that his father was the sun, his mother was the moon, and his eleven brothers were the eleven stars. This is confirmed in Revelation 12:1.

> *"And there appeared a great wonder in heaven; a woman clothed with the sun, and the moon under her feet, and upon her head a crown of twelve stars;"*

This woman clothed with the sun, and the moon under her feet and which had upon her head a crown of twelve stars, is this. The woman represents the land of Israel, and again the sun is the father Jacob who was later name Israel by God, and the moon represents Rachael, the wife of Jacob. The eleven stars in Genesis 37:9-11 are now twelve stars because Joseph is being counted. It now represents all twelve tribes or sons of Israel. Joseph was rejected but not forsaken. Just because people reject God's chosen ones, does not mean that they are forsaken. God called us to be "**above and not beneath, to be the head and not the tail**." In the end, God's chosen ones, will one day soon, inherit this world.

The Mystery Of
Who Will Be Given Knowledge

In the book of Isaiah 28:9-13, there is a very important mystery that everyone should pray to God to understand.

> *"Whom shall he <u>teach knowledge</u>? and whom shall he <u>make to understand doctrine</u>? them that are weaned from the milk, and drawn from the breasts. For precept must be upon precept, precept upon precept; line upon line, line upon line; here a little, and there a little: For with <u>stammering lips and another tongue will he speak to this people</u>. To whom he said, This is the rest wherewith ye may cause the <u>weary to rest</u>; and this is the <u>refreshing</u>: yet they would not hear. But the word of the Lord was unto them precept upon precept, precept; upon precept; line upon line line upon line; here a little and there a little, that they might go, and fall backward, and be broken, and snared, and taken."*

There are two groups of people that are being talked to in this passage of scriptures. Those that He is going to give knowledge and doctrine to, who are blessed, and the other group, which is called "They", who would not listen to what the first group was saying. God is talking about His doctrine, and He is saying that He is going to give it to them that have been **"weaned from the milk"**, babes in Christ, and newly born people in the body of Christ.

> *"For every one that useth milk is unskilful in the word of righteousness: for he is a babe"*—Hebrews 5:13

> *"Wherefore laying aside all malice, and all guile, and hypocrisies, and envies, and all evil speakings, As newborn babes, desire the sincere milk of the word, that ye may grow thereby: If so be ye have tasted that the Lord is gracious."*—I Peter 2:1-3

God is giving the knowledge of His doctrine to His children so they can grow up. Then in Isaiah 28:10 it is said that these people had to study to show themselves approved unto God. Then he said in verse 11, "**with stammering lips and another tongue will he speak to this people**. *That* **"This is the rest Wherewith ye may cause the weary to rest;"** That this is also the "**refreshing**" that you will only find in the tongues. It is the Holy Ghost. There are those that say that tongues have ceased, that there is no more use for it, and use this scripture to justify them self.

> *"**Charity never faileth: but whether there be prophecies, they shall fail; whether there be tongues, they shall cease; whether be knowledge, it shall vanish away.**"*—I Corinthians 13:8

I wonder why out of all four of these things, the only one satin want to get rid of in this last church age (Laodiceans) is the tongues. Every thing else is still at work according to some. But that is not the case. The Comforter is for every one that wants to be saved and it comes speaking "**with other tongues.**"

> *"For the promise is unto you, and to your children, and to <u>all that are afar off</u>, even as many as the Lord our God shall call."*—The Acts 2:39

> *"And there appeared unto them cloven tongues like as of fire, and it sat upon each of them. And they were all filled with the Holy Ghost, and began to speak with other tongues, as the Spirit gave them utterance."*—Acts 2:3-4

> *"Therefore let all the house of Israel know assuredly, that God hath made that same Jesus, whom ye have crucified, both Lord and Christ. Now when they heard this, they were pricked in their heart, and said unto Peter and to the*

> *rest of the apostles, Men and brethren, what shall we do? Then Peter said unto them, Repent, and be baptized every one of you in the name of Jesus Christ for the remission of sins, and ye shall receive the gift of the Holy Ghost. For the <u>promise</u> is unto <u>you</u>, and to <u>your children</u>, and to <u>all</u> that are <u>afar off</u>, even <u>as many as the</u> <u>LORD our God shall call</u>"*—Acts 2:36-39

God has to call you, because none of us is worthy to be saved. I often ask myself, "Why did he desire me?" I always felt that there were others in my family that were more deserving than I, but I found out this,

> *"For all have sinned, and come short of the glory of God;"*—Romans 3:23

I found out later that Jesus had promised the world the Comforter if they believed in his word.

> *"But when the <u>Comforter</u> is come, whom <u>I will send unto you from the</u> <u>Father</u>, <u>even the Spirit of truth</u>, which proceedeth from the Father, he shall <u>testify of me</u>: And ye also shall bear witness, because ye have been with me from the beginning."*—St. John 15:26-27

> *"To whom he said, <u>This is the rest</u> wherewith ye may cause the weary to rest; and this is the refreshing: yet they would not hear."*—Isaiah 28:12

This verse is saying to His people, tell others that "**This is the rest wherewith ye may cause the weary to rest.**" The only true rest can only be found in Jesus Christ and in the Holy Ghost. Note **This** start with a capitol **T** which means that it is speaking of Gods Holy Spirit. Every ones rest can only be found in the Holy Ghost.

> *"Come unto me, all ye that labor and are heavy laden, and I will give you <u>rest.</u> Take my yoke upon you, and learn of me; for I am meek and lowly in heart: and ye shall find <u>rest unto your souls.</u> For my yoke is easy, and my burden is light".*—St. Matthew 11:28-30

> *"Wherefore (as the Holy Ghost saith, today if ye will hear <u>his voice</u>, Harden not your hearts, as in the provocation, in the day of temptation in the wilderness: When your fathers tempted me, proved me, and saw my works forty years. Wherefore I was grieved with that generation, and said, They do always err in their heart; and <u>they have not known my ways</u>. So I sware in my wrath, They shall not enter into my <u>rest</u>.)"*—Hebrews 3:7-11

This is the refreshing, yet people will not receive what the first group of people is saying, know, and have witnessed. Their studying become in vain because they did not obtain the stammering lips and other tongues that the others received.

> *"But the word of the Lord was unto them precept upon precept, precept upon precept; line upon line, line upon line; here a little, and there a little; that they might go and fall backward, and be broken, and snared, and taken."*—Isaiah 28:13

In other words, this meant that they are going to study just like the first group, but will not rightly divide the word and therefore, will not find a place in the Holy Ghost, to rest. They rejected the refreshing, they discarded the tongues, and by doing so it caused them to **"fall backward and be broken, and snared."** They will be taken by Satan in the end because they did not accept the **"stammering lips and another tongue"** which God prophesied of before.

> *"And it shall come to pass afterward, that I will pour out my spirit upon all flesh; and your sons and your daughters shall prophesy, your old men shall dream dreams, your young men shall see visions: And also upon the servants and upon the handmaids in those days will I pour out my spirit."*—Joel 2:28-29

> *"And they were all filled with the Holy Ghost, and began to speak with other tongues, as the Spirit gave them utterance."*—Acts 2:4

The wisdom and knowledge of God's doctrine was given to the Gentile nation in Acts 8:26-39.

> *"And the angel of the Lord spake unto Philip, saying, Arise, and go toward the south unto the way that goeth down from Jerusalem unto Gaza, which is desert. And he arose and went: and, behold, a man of Ethiopia, an eunuch of great authority under Candace queen of the Ethiopians, who had the charge of all her treasure, and had come to Jerusalem for to worship, Was returning, and sitting in his chariot read Esaias the prophet. Then the Spirit said unto Philip, Go near, and join thyself to this chariot. And Philip ran thither to him, and heard him read the prophet Esaias and said, Understandest thou what thou readest? And he said, How can I, except some man should guide me? And he desired Philip that he would come up and sit with him. The place of the scripture which he read was this, He was led as a sheep to the slaughter; and like a lamb dumb before his shearer, so opened he not his mouth: In his humiliation his judgment was taken away: and who shall declare his generation? for his life is taken from the earth. And the eunuch answered Philip, and said, I pray thee, of whom speaketh the prophet this? of himself, or of some other man? Then Philip opened his mouth, and began at the same scripture, and preached unto him Jesus. And as they went on their way, they came unto a certain water: and the eunuch said, See, here is water; what doth hinder me to be baptized? And Philip said, If thou believest with all thine heart, thou mayest. And he answered and said, I believe that Jesus Christ is the Son of God. And he commanded the chariot to stand still: and they went down both into the water; both Philip and the eunuch; and he baptized him. And when they were come up out of the water, the Spirit of the Lord caught away Philip that the eunuch saw him no more: and he went on his way rejoicing."*

After this the Holy Ghost gave the hidden mystery of tongues to Cornelius, a centurion of the Italian band and officer in the army.

"There was a certain man in Caesarea called Cornelius, a centurion of the band called the Italian band, A devout man, and one that feared God with all his house, which gave much alms to the people, and prayed to God always. He saw in a vision evidently about the ninth hour of the day an angel of God coming in to him, and saying unto him, Cornelius. And when he looked on him, he was afraid, and said, What is it, Lord? And he said unto him, Thy prayers and thine alms are come up for a memorial before God. And now send men to Joppa, and call for one Simon, whose surname is Peter: He lodgeth with one Simon a tanner, whose house is by the sea side: he shall tell thee what thou oughtest to do. And when the angel which spake unto Cornelius was departed, he called two of his household servants, and a devout soldier of them that waited on him continually; And when he had declared all these things unto them, he sent them to Joppa."—Acts 10:1-8

Peter was given a vision by God concerning Cornelius who was also a Gentile. The vision that Peter had was this.

"On the morrow, as they went on their journey, and drew nigh unto the city, Peter went up upon the housetop to pray about the sixth hour: And he became very hungry, and would have eaten: but while they made ready, he fell into a trance, And saw heaven opened, and a certain vessel descending unto him, as it had been a great sheet knit at the four corners, and let down to the earth: Wherein were all manner of fourfooted beasts of the earth, and wild beasts, and creeping things, and fowls of the air. And there came a voice to him, Rise, Peter; kill, and eat. But Peter said, Not so, Lord; for I have never eaten any thing that is common or unclean. And the voice spake unto him again the second time, What God hath cleansed, that call not thou common. This was done thrice: and the vessel was received up again into heaven."—Acts 10:9-16

God revealed to Peter that He was going to save the Gentile nations. He told Peter not to call those He had cleansed, unclean or common. The variety of beasts, creeping things, and fowls of the air, all represented us, the people of the Gentile nations. There are those who exhibit a beastly personality, people that creep around; always in someone else's business, people who think they are better than others; who walk around, with their noses in the air and because of a position, or education, place themselves in a category above the rest. I am sure that you have met with one of these personality types at some point in your life. But God has no respect of person, He loves us all.

The Jewish nation viewed Gentiles in this manner, they believed themselves to be better than Gentiles. However, when Peter and his friends followed the men that were sent to retrieve him by the order of Cornelius, they found that God's love extended to the Gentiles as well.

"This was done thrice: and the vessel was received up again into heaven. Now while Peter doubted in himself what this vision which he had seen should mean, behold, the men which were sent from Cornelius had made inquiry for Simon's house, and stood before the gate, And called, and asked whether Simon, which was surnamed Peter, were lodged there. While Peter thought on the vision, the Spirit said unto him, Behold, three men seek thee. Arise therefore, and get thee down, and go with them, doubting nothing: for I have sent them. Then Peter went down to the men which were sent unto him from Cornelius; and said, Behold, I am he whom ye seek: what is the cause wherefore ye are come? And they said, Cornelius the centurion, a just man, and one that feareth God, and of good report among all the nation of the Jews, was warned from God by an holy angel to send for thee into his house, and to hear words of thee. Then called he them in, and lodged them. And on the morrow Peter went away with them, and certain brethren from Joppa accompanied him. And the morrow after they entered into Caesarea. And Cornelius waited for them, and had called together his kinsmen and near friends. And as Peter was coming in, Cornelius met him, and fell down at his feet, and worshipped him. But Peter took him up, saying, Stand up; I myself also am a man. And as he talked with him, he went in, and found many that were come

together. And he said unto them, Ye know how that it is an unlawful thing for a man that is a Jew to keep company, or come unto one of another nation; but God hath showed me that I should not call any man common or unclean. Therefore came I unto you without gainsaying, as soon as I was sent for: I ask therefore for what intent ye have sent for me? And Cornelius said, Four days ago I was fasting until this hour; and at the ninth hour I prayed in my house, and, behold, a man stood before me in bright clothing, And said, Cornelius, thy prayer is heard, and thine alms are had in remembrance in the sight of God. Send therefore to Joppa, and call hither Simon, whose surname is Peter; he is lodged in the house of one Simon a tanner by the sea side: who, when he cometh, shall speak unto thee. Immediately therefore I sent to thee; and thou hast well done that thou art come. Now therefore are we all here present before God, to hear all things that are commanded thee of God. Then Peter opened his mouth, and said, Of a truth I perceive that God is no respecter of persons: But in every nation he that feareth him, and worketh righteousness, is accepted with him. The word which God sent unto the children of Israel, preaching peace by Jesus Christ: (he is Lord of all:) That word, I say, ye know, which was published throughout all Judaea, and began from Galilee, after the baptism which John preached; How God anointed Jesus of Nazareth with the Holy Ghost and with power: who went about doing good, and healing all that were oppressed of the devil; for God was with him. And we are witnesses of all things which he did both in the land of the Jews, and in Jerusalem; whom they slew and hanged on a tree: Him God raised up the third day, and showed him openly; Not to all the people, but unto witnesses chosen before God, even to us, who did eat and drink with him after he rose from the dead. And he commanded us to preach unto the people, and to testify that it is he which was ordained of God to be the Judge of quick and dead. To him give all the prophets witness, that through his name whosoever believeth in him shall receive remission of sins. While Peter yet spake these words, the Holy Ghost fell on all them which heard the word. And they of the circumcision which believed were astonished, as many as came with Peter, because that on the Gentiles also was poured out the gift of the Holy Ghost. For they heard them speak with tongues, and magnify God. Then answered Peter, Can any man forbid water, that these should not be baptized, which have received the Holy Ghost as well as we? And he commanded them to be baptized in the name of the Lord. Then prayed they him to tarry certain days. And the apostles and brethren that were in Judaea heard that the Gentiles had also received the word of God. And when Peter was come up to Jerusalem, they that were of the circumcision contended with him, Saying, Thou wentest in to men uncircumcised, and didst eat with them. But Peter rehearsed the matter from the beginning, and expounded it by order unto them, saying, I was in the city of Joppa praying: and in a trance I saw a vision, A certain vessel descend, as it had been a great sheet, let down from heaven by four corners; and it came even to me: Upon the which when I had fastened mine eyes, I considered, and saw fourfooted beasts of the earth, and wild beasts, and creeping things, and fowls of the air. And I heard a voice saying unto me, Arise, Peter; slay and eat. But I said, Not so, Lord: for nothing common or unclean hath at any time entered into my mouth. But the voice answered me again from heaven, What God hath cleansed, that call not thou common. And this was done three times: and all were drawn up again into heaven. And, behold, immediately there were three men already come unto the house where I was, sent from Caesarea unto me. And the Spirit bade me go with them, nothing doubting. Moreover these six brethren accompanied me, and we entered into the man's house: And he showed us how he had seen an angel in his house, which stood and said unto him, Send men to Joppa, and call for Simon, whose surname is Peter; Who shall tell thee words, whereby thou and all thy house shall be saved. And as I began to speak, the Holy Ghost fell on them, as on us at the beginning. Then remembered I the word of the Lord, how that he said, John indeed baptized with water; but ye shall be baptized with the Holy Ghost.

Forasmuch then as God gave them the like gift as he did unto us, who believed on the Lord Jesus Christ; what was I, that I could withstand God? When they heard these things, they held their peace, and glorified God, saying, Then hath God also to the Gentiles granted repentance unto life."—Acts 10:16-11:18

"I the LORD have called thee in righteousness, and will hold thine hand, and will keep thee, and give thee for a covenant of the people, for a light of the Gentiles; To open the blind eyes, to bring out the prisoners from the prison, and them that sit in darkness out of the prison house."—Isaiah 42:6-7

The passages of scripture you just read are talking about God's calling on Jesus, to be given as a covenant of the people and a light for the Gentiles. We were all in the prison of darkness. We did not know about the Christ who came into the world that we might be saved and brought out of the prison houses, and out of the darkness that is in this world. He gave us a choice of staying in that darkness or coming into His marvelous light.

Mystery Of The Sons Of God

"And it came to pass, when men began to multiply on the face of the earth, and daughters were born unto them, That <u>the sons of God</u> saw the daughters of men that they were fair; and they took them wives of all which they chose". And the LORD said, "My spirit shall not always strive with <u>man</u>, for that <u>he also is flesh</u>: yet <u>his days</u> shall be an hundred and twenty years. There were giants in the earth in those days; and also after that, <u>when the sons of God</u> came in unto the daughters of men, and <u>they bare children to them</u>, the same became mighty men which were of old, men of renown. And God saw that the wickedness of man was great in the earth, and that every imagination of the thoughts of his heart was only evil continually. And it <u>repented the LORD that he had made man</u> on the earth, and it grieved him at his heart. And the LORD said, I will destroy <u>man</u> whom I have created from the face of the earth; both man, and beast, and the creeping thing, and the fowls of the air; for it repenteth me that I have made them. But <u>Noah found grace</u> in the eyes of the LORD. These are the generations of Noah: Noah was a just man and perfect in his generations, and <u>Noah walked with God</u>. And Noah begat three sons, Shem, Ham, and Japheth. The earth also was corrupt before God, and the earth was filled with violence. And God looked upon the earth, and, behold, it was corrupt; for all flesh had corrupted his way upon the earth. And God said unto

Noah, The end of all flesh is come before me; for the earth is filled with violence through them; and, behold, I will destroy them with the earth. Make thee an ark of gopher wood; rooms shalt thou make in the ark, and shalt pitch it within and without with pitch. And this is the fashion which thou shalt make it of: The length of the ark shall be three hundred cubits, the breadth of it fifty cubits, and the height of it thirty cubits. A window shalt thou make to the ark, and in a cubit shalt thou finish it above; and the door of the ark shalt thou set in the side thereof; with lower, second, and third stories shalt thou make it. And, behold, I, even I, do bring a flood of waters upon the earth, to destroy all flesh, wherein is the breath of life, from under heaven; and every thing that is in the earth shall die. But with thee will I establish my covenant; and thou shalt come into the ark, thou, and thy sons, and thy wife, and thy sons' wives with thee. And of every living thing of all flesh, two of every sort shalt thou bring into the ark, to keep them alive with thee; they shall be male and female. Of fowls after their kind, and of cattle after their kind, of every creeping thing of the earth after his kind, two of every sort shall come unto thee, to keep them alive. And take thou unto thee of all food that is eaten, and thou shalt gather it to thee; and it shall be for food for thee, and for them. Thus did Noah; according to all that God commanded him, so did he."—Genesis 6:1-22

These scriptures deals with the generation of the first Adam.

"The first man is of the earth, earthy: the second man is the Lord from heaven."—I Corinthians 15:47

It is important to remember this because there are two schools of thought in this chapter. As you read in the generations of Adam, I would have you to note that two descendants are mentioned. Abel who represented the sons of God, the just sons, and Cain who represented the sons of man, the unjust, (The saint and the sinner.) The sons of men felt that they were not subject to the word of God. They continue today as at the first, disobedient to God's word, after the likeness of Cain. But Abel was replaced by another son, to represent the child of God's side. His name was Seth.

> *"And Adam lived an hundred and thirty years, and begat a son in his own likeness, after his image; and called his name Seth:"*—Genesis 5:3

God was known as Jehovah to Adam, Eve, Cain and Abel until the death of Abel who represented good and obedience. Man stopped calling on the name Jehovah until the birth of Enos who was the good and obedient side of the family. God was well pleased with the birth of Enos and at that time men began once more to call on the name of Jehovah.

> *"And Adam knew his wife again; and she bare a son, and called his name Seth: For God, said she, hath appointed me another seed instead of Abel, whom Cain slew. And to Seth, to him also there was born a son; and he called his name Enos: then began men to call upon the name of the LORD."*—Genesis 4:25-26

Some time between Enos and Terah son of Abram (Abraham), men once again stopped calling God by the name of Jehovah, until Moses.

> *"And God spake unto Moses, and said unto him, I am the LORD: And I appeared unto Abraham, unto Isaac, and unto Jacob, by the name of God Almighty, but by my name JEHOVAH was I not known to them."*—Exodus 6:2-3

In Genesis 6, it tells how man began to multiply on the face of the earth. It then speaks of the daughters that were born unto the sons of men and how the sons of God saw their beauty and began to marry these daughters of men, who did not believe nor were subject to the word of God, as their father Cain was not.

The other school of thought is that the sons of God were angels and the daughters of men were human beings who came together and brought forth giants. That is not so.

> *"And the LORD said, My spirit shall not always strive with <u>man</u>, for that he also is flesh: yet his days shall be an hundred and twenty years."*—Genesis 6:3

God was angry with the sons of God because they had become disobedient and allowed their flesh to dictate to them more than God's word, for they began to mingle with and marry sinners. God then sentenced mankind because of their flesh and disobedience. God clearly states in the following scriptures that it was men, **NOT** angels that went into the daughters of men. These sons of God were men of God, like you and I, who were God's children.

> *"There were giants in the earth in those days; and also after that, when the sons of God came in unto the daughters of men, and they bare children to them, the same became mighty men which were of old, men of renown. And God saw that the wickedness of <u>man</u> was great in the earth, and that every imagination of the thoughts of his heart was only evil continually. And it repented the LORD that he had made <u>man</u> on the earth, and it grieved him at his heart. And the LORD said, I will destroy <u>man</u> whom I have created from the face of the earth; both <u>man</u>, and beast, and the creeping thing, and the fowls of the air; for it repenteth me that I have made them."*—Genesis 6:4-7

In those days, out of all the sons of God, four remained. Noah and his sons whom he had brought up in the way they should go, Ham, Shem, and Japheth, along with their wives. They were the only ones who found grace in the eyes of the Lord.

Of these three sons of Noah, Japheth was the first born.

> *"Unto Shem also, the father of all the children of Eber, the brother of Japheth the <u>elder</u>, even to him were children born."*—Genesis 10:21

Ham was the youngest of the three sons.

> *"These are the three sons of Noah: and of them was the whole earth overspread. And Noah began to be an husbandman, and he planted a vineyard: And he drank of the wine, and was drunken; and he was uncovered within his tent. And Ham, the father of Canaan, saw the nakedness of his father, and told his two brethren without. And Shem and Japheth took a garment, and laid it upon*

both their shoulders, and went backward, and covered the nakedness of their father; and their faces were backward, and they saw not their father's nakedness. And Noah awoke from his wine, and knew what his <u>younger</u> son had done unto him."—Genesis 9:19-24

This leaves Shem to be the middle child, but they are **TRIPLETS**, all born when Noah was five hundred years old.

"And Noah was five hundred years old: and Noah begat Shem, Ham, and Japheth."—Genesis 5:32

"And Noah began to be an husbandman, and he planted a vineyard: And he drank of the wine, and was drunken; and he was uncovered within his tent. And Ham, the father of Canaan, saw the nakedness of his father, and told his two brethren without. And Shem and Japheth took a garment, and laid it upon both their shoulders, and went backward, and covered the nakedness of their father; and their faces were backward, and they saw not their father's nakedness. And Noah awoke from his wine, and knew what his younger son had done unto him. And he said, Cursed be Canaan; a servant of servants shall he be unto his brethren. And he said, Blessed be the Lord God of Shem; and Canaan shall be his servant. God shall enlarge Japheth, and he shall dwell in the tents of Shem; and Canaan shall be his servant."-Genesis 9:20-27

There were those that tried to use this passage of scripture as an excuse to justify enslaving a people, and to treat them as if they were not human, as if they did not have souls. This curse that took place above was not honored by God because Noah was drunk and out of his mind. God did not honor this intoxicated curse from a man whose mind had been altered by strong drink. This curse never came to pass. Instead of Ham becoming the servant of Shem, Shem was the servant of Ham in Egypt, under the rule of the Pharaohs, for over four hundred years until their exodus. Then he was freed by God. This was the beginning of Shem's rule, under the leadership of King Solomon.

"And it came to pass, that at midnight the LORD smote all the firstborn in the land of Egypt, from the firstborn of Pharaoh that sat on his throne unto the firstborn of the captive that was in the dungeon; and all the firstborn of cattle. And Pharaoh rose up in the night, he, and all his servants, and all the Egyptians; and there was a great cry in Egypt; for there was not a house where there was not one dead. And he called for Moses and Aaron by night, and said, Rise up, and get you forth from among my people, both ye and the children of Israel; and go, serve the LORD, as ye have said."—Exodus 12:29-31

The Dream Of The Terrible Image

In the book of Daniel chapter 2, it tells us that in the second year of the reign of Nebuchadnezzar, he had a dream of great significance. It was a dream of what was going to take place in the latter days. This dream was dealing with the elder son of Noah, Japheth, who is the father of the white race. He was the last son of Noah that was given the key of knowledge and wisdom. The last opportunity for one of Noah's sons to bring in righteous government was placed upon him. The other two sons, Ham and Shem, had their chance to do so but failed. The fact that Jesus is coming back to set up righteous government tells us that Japheth failed also. All we need for proof of Japheth failure is to look around.

> *"For unto us a child is born, unto us a son is given: and the government shall be upon his shoulder: and his name shall be called Wonderful, Counsellor, The mighty God, The everlasting Father, The Prince of Peace. Of the increase of his government and peace there shall be no end, upon the throne of David, and upon his kingdom, to order it, and to establish it with judgment and with justice from henceforth even for ever. The zeal of the LORD of hosts will perform this."*—Isaiah 9:6-7

This image's reign was going to be a **bright** and **excellent reign**. This image symbolized the reign of the last son. It was also said to be a **terrible image**, and a **terrible reign**. Its form consists of a combination of bright and bad qualities which made it what it would be.

"The king answered and said to Daniel, whose name was Belteshazzar, Art thou able to make known unto me the dream which I have seen, and the interpretation thereof? Daniel answered in the presence of the king, and said, The secret which the king hath demanded cannot the wise men, the astrologers, the magicians, the soothsayers, show unto the king; But there is a God in heaven that revealeth secrets, and maketh known to the king Nebuchadnezzar what shall be in the latter days. Thy dream, and the visions of thy head upon thy bed, are these; As for thee, O king, thy thoughts came into thy mind upon thy bed, what should come to pass hereafter: and he that revealeth secrets maketh known to thee what shall come to pass. But as for me, this secret is not revealed to me for any wisdom that I have more than any living, but for their sakes that shall make known the interpretation to the king, and that thou mightest know the thoughts of thy heart. Thou, O king, sawest, and behold a great image. This great image, whose brightness was excellent, stood before thee; and the form thereof was terrible. This image's head was of fine gold, his breast and his arms of silver, his belly and his thighs of brass, His legs of iron, his feet part of iron and part of clay. Thou sawest till that a stone was cut out without hands, which smote the image upon his feet that were of iron and clay, and brake them to pieces. Then was the iron, the clay, the brass, the silver, and the gold, broken to pieces together, and became like the chaff of the summer threshingfloors; and the wind carried them away, that no place was found for them: and the stone that smote the image became a great mountain, and filled the whole earth. This is the dream; and we will tell the interpretation thereof before the king. Thou, O king, art a king of kings: for the God of heaven hath given thee a kingdom, power, and strength, and glory. And wheresoever the children of men dwell, the beasts of the field and the fowls of the heaven hath he given into thine hand, and hath made thee ruler over them all. Thou art this head of gold."—Daniel 2:26-38

This image's head of gold was the beginning of Japheth's reign. This head of gold was Nebuchadnezzar, whose kingdom was eventually defeated by the next part of that image's body. I will have you to note that the movement is descending always toward the feet which represents the last state of the body, of this image, which represents **The Ten Toe Kingdom**. Also you should notice that the "His" in legs is the only one that began with a capital letter, which should tell you something.

The next part of that body represented the Medes and Persians which represent the arms and breast joined together to defeat Nebuchadnezzar's Kingdom. The leaders of these two kingdoms were Darius and Cyrus. The next descending kingdom following those kingdoms, was the kingdom of Grecia, lead by a mighty Greek leader by the name of **Alexander the Great.**

> *"And now will I show thee the truth. Behold, there shall stand up yet three kings in Persia; and the fourth shall be far richer than they all: and by his strength through his riches he shall stir up all against the realm of Grecia. And a mighty king shall stand up, that shall rule with great dominion, and do according to his will. And when he shall stand up, his kingdom shall be broken, and shall be divided toward the four winds of heaven; and not to his posterity, nor according to his dominion which he ruled: for his kingdom shall be plucked up, even for others beside those."*—Daniel 11:2-4

Shortly after he had conquered Mede and Persia, he died and his kingdom was split into four parts by his four generals. It became the Roman Empire. Alexander's kingdom was the belly and thighs of brass in this image. Then came the legs, which represent Rome. Last but not least, the feet of this image which you do not want to be a part of, for there will be at this time a time of trouble as never was before. A time when everyone in order to survive must take on the sign of the beast . . . . **SIX, SIX, SIX**. Without it, you will not be able to buy or sell. There is no body of the image after that. This kingdom is the one where Satan's spirit will be in the body of a man, and he shall rule for seven years. That man will be the anti-Christ. The second half of his rule will be one of horror for the saints left behind, 144,000 of them. He will make war with them until he is allowed by God to kill them all.

> *"But pray ye that your flight be not in the winter, neither on the sabbath day: For then shall be great tribulation, such as was not since the beginning of the world to this time, no, nor ever shall be. And except those days should be shortened, there should no flesh be saved: but for the elect's sake those days shall be shortened. Then if any man shall say unto you, Lo, here is Christ, or there; believe it not. For there shall arise false Christs, and false prophets, and shall show great signs and wonders; insomuch that, if it were possible, they shall deceive the very elect. Behold, I have told you before. Wherefore if they shall say unto you, Behold, he is in the desert; go not forth: behold, he is in the secret chambers; believe it not."*—St. Matthew—24:20-26

> *"Ask ye now, and see whether a man doth travail with child? wherefore do I see every man with his hands on his loins, as a woman in travail, and all faces are turned into paleness? Alas! for that day is great, so that none is like it: it is even the time of Jacob's trouble; but he shall be saved out of it."*—Jeremiah 30:6-7

After the anti-Christ and Satan kill them, God is going to bring them back to life as the completion of His heavenly army. Flight is speaking of the Rapture, winter and Sabbath day is symbolic of *last* in this verse. You do not want to be left down here to take that last flight if you are a Gentile because that flight is already booked for Jews and the cost of the ticket is your death.

> *"And I saw another angel ascending from the east, having the seal of the living God: and he cried with a loud voice to the four angels, to whom it was given to hurt the earth and the sea, Saying, Hurt not the earth, neither the sea, nor the trees, till we have sealed the servants of our God in their foreheads. And I heard the number of them which were sealed: and there were sealed an hundred and forty and four thousand of all the tribes of the children of Israel. Of the tribe of Judah were sealed twelve thousand. Of the tribe of Reuben were sealed twelve thousand. Of*

> *the tribe of Gad were sealed twelve thousand. Of the tribe of Aser were sealed twelve thousand. Of the tribe of Nephthalim were sealed twelve thousand. Of the tribe of Manasses were sealed twelve thousand. Of the tribe of Simeon were sealed twelve thousand. Of the tribe of Levi were sealed twelve thousand. Of the tribe of Issachar were sealed twelve thousand. Of the tribe of Zabulon were sealed twelve thousand. Of the tribe of Joseph were sealed twelve thousand. Of the tribe of Benjamin were sealed twelve thousand."*—Revelation 7:2-8

> *"And I looked, and, lo, a Lamb stood on the mount Zion, and with him an hundred forty and four thousand, having his Father's name written in their foreheads. And I heard a voice from heaven, as the voice of many waters, and as the voice of a great thunder: and I heard the voice of harpers harping with their harps: And they sung as it were a new song before the throne, and before the four beasts, and the elders: and no man could learn that song but the hundred and forty and four thousand, which were redeemed from the earth. These are they which were not defiled with women; for they are virgins. These are they which follow the Lamb whithersoever he goeth. These were redeemed from among men, being the firstfruits unto God and to the Lamb. And in their mouth was found no guile: for they are without fault before the throne of God."*—Revelation 14:1-5

Jesus is going to come and set up righteous government and bring to an end the anti-Christ's and Satan's reign over the world.

> *"And whereas thou sawest the feet and toes, part of potters' clay, and part of iron, the kingdom shall be divided; but there shall be in it of the strength of the iron, forasmuch as thou sawest the iron mixed with miry clay. And as the toes of the feet were part of iron, and part of clay, so the kingdom shall be partly strong, and partly broken. And whereas thou sawest iron mixed with miry clay, they shall mingle themselves with the seed of men: but they shall not cleave one to another, even as iron is not mixed with clay.*

And in the days of these kings shall the God of heaven set up a kingdom, which shall never be destroyed: and the kingdom shall not be left to other people, but it shall break in pieces and consume all these kingdoms, and it shall stand for ever."—Daniel 2:41-44

"And at that time shall Michael stand up, the great prince which standeth for the children of thy people: and there shall be a time of trouble, such as never was since there was a nation even to that same time: and at that time thy people shall be delivered, every one that shall be found written in the book. And many of them that sleep in the dust of the earth shall awake, some to everlasting life, and some to shame and everlasting contempt. And they that be wise shall shine as the brightness of the firmament; and they that turn many to righteousness as the stars for ever and ever. But thou, O Daniel, shut up the words, and seal the book, even to the time of the end: many shall run to and fro, and knowedge shall be increased."—Daniel 12:1-4

"And I heard, but I understood not: then said I, O my Lord, what shall be the end of these things? And he said, Go thy way, Daniel: for the words are closed up and sealed till the time of the end. Many shall be purified, and made white, and tried; but the wicked shall do wickedly: and none of the wicked shall understand; but the wise shall understand."—Daniel 12:8-10

Many shall be cleansed of their sins, and saved. They will go through trials and tribulations; but the sinners shall become more wicked.

"And I saw the beast, and the kings of the earth, and their armies, gathered together to make war against him that sat on the horse, and against his army. And the beast was taken, and with him the false prophet that wrought miracles before him, with which he deceived them that had received the mark of the beast, and them that worshipped his image. These both were cast alive into a lake of fire

burning with brimstone. And the remnant were slain with the sword of him that sat upon the horse, which sword proceeded out of his mouth: and all the fowls were filled with their flesh."—Revelation 19:19-21

If this is understood now, it only means that we are at the time of the end.

The Vision Of The Seventy Weeks

These seventy weeks represent not days, but years. Each week is made up of seven years and not seven days. It is important to the Gentile people to know what this seventy week period means to them, because at the end of it there will no longer be sin for a while. In Daniel there is something that is known as **"standing in the gap."**

> *"And whiles I was speaking, and praying, and confessing my sin and the sin of my people Israel, and presenting my supplication before the LORD my God for the holy mountain of my God; Yea, whiles I was speaking in prayer, even the man Gabriel, whom I had seen in the vision at the beginning, being caused to fly swiftly, touched me about the time of the evening oblation. And he informed me, and talked with me, and said, O Daniel, I am now come forth to give thee skill and understanding. At the beginning of thy supplications the commandment came forth, and I am come to show thee; for thou art greatly beloved: therefore understand the matter, and consider the vision. Seventy weeks are determined upon thy people and upon thy holy city, to finish the transgression, and to make an end of sins, and to make reconciliation for iniquity, and to bring in everlasting righteousness, and to seal up the vision and prophecy, and to anoint the most Holy. Know therefore and understand, that from the going forth of the commandment to restore and to build Jerusalem unto the Messiah the Prince shall be seven weeks, and threescore and two weeks: the street shall be built again, and the*

wall, even in troublous times. And after threescore and two weeks shall Messiah be cut off, but not for himself: and the people of the prince that shall come shall destroy the city and the sanctuary; and the end thereof shall be with a flood, and unto the end of the war desolations are determined. And he shall confirm the covenant with many for one week: and in the midst of the week he shall cause the sacrifice and the oblation to cease, and for the overspreading of abominations he shall make it desolate, even until the consummation, and that determined shall be poured upon the desolate."—Daniel 9:20-27

It deals with the Gentiles' salvation.

"On the morrow, as they went on their journey, and drew nigh unto the city, Peter went up upon the housetop to pray about the sixth hour: And he became very hungry, and would have eaten: but while they made ready, he fell into a trance, And saw heaven opened, and a certain vessel descending unto him, as it had been a great sheet knit at the four corners, and let down to the earth: Wherein were all manner of fourfooted beasts of the earth, and wild beasts, and creeping things, and fowls of the air. And there came a voice to him, Rise, Peter; kill, and eat. But Peter said, Not so, Lord; for I have never eaten any thing that is common or unclean. And the voice spake unto him again the second time, What God hath cleansed, that call not thou common."—Acts 10:9-15

"While Peter yet spake these words, the Holy Ghost fell on all them which heard the word. And they of the circumcision which believed were astonished, as many as came with Peter, because that on the Gentiles also was poured out the gift of the Holy Ghost. For they heard them speak with tongues, and magnify God. Then answered Peter, Can any man forbid water, that these should not be baptized, which have received the Holy Ghost as well as we? And he commanded them to be baptized in the name of the Lord. Then prayed they him to tarry certain days."—Acts 10:44-48

If those seventy weeks would have been fulfilled, the Gentile nations would have been left out of God's salvation plan. But thanks be to God, we were not left out of the olive tree. We were that wild olive tree that was not a part of God's olive tree which consisted of only Jews. We were added between the sixty ninth week and the last week, which is the seventieth week. The Gentile nations can not and will not be saved in that last week. The Jews at that time are the only ones being grafted in.

> *"For I speak to you Gentiles, inasmuch as I am the apostle of the Gentiles, I magnify mine office: If by any means I may provoke to emulation them which are my flesh, and might save some of them. For if the casting away of them be the reconciling of the world, what shall the receiving of them be, but life from the dead? For if the firstfruit be holy, the lump is also holy: and if the root be holy, so are the branches. And if some of the branches be broken off, and thou, being a wild olive tree, wert grafted in among them, and with them partakest of the root and fatness of the olive tree; Boast not against the branches. But if thou boast, thou bearest not the root, but the root thee. Thou wilt say then, The branches were broken off, that I might be grafted in. Well; because of unbelief they were broken off, and thou standest by faith. Be not highminded, but fear: For if God spared not the natural branches, take heed lest he also spare not thee. Behold therefore the goodness and severity of God: on them which fell, severity; but toward thee, goodness, if thou continue in his goodness: otherwise thou also shalt be cut off. And they also, if they abide not still in unbelief, shall be grafted in: for God is able to graft them in again. For if thou wert cut out of the olive tree which is wild by nature, and wert grafted contrary to nature into a good olive tree: how much more shall these, which be the natural branches, be grafted into their own olive tree? For I would not, brethren, that ye should be ignorant of this mystery, lest ye should be wise in your own conceits; that blindness in part is happened to Israel, <u>until the fulness of the Gentiles</u> be come in."*—Romans 11:13-25

At the end of the sixty-ninth week, the Messiah, Jesus Christ, the prince, died. Not just for his people the Jews, but for the Gentile race as well. He now stands in the gap holding off the seventieth week, saying to all of the Gentile nations,

> *"Come unto me, all ye that labour and are heavy laden, and I will give you rest. Take my yoke upon you, and learn of me; for I am meek and lowly in heart: and ye shall find rest unto your souls. For my yoke is easy, and my burden is light."*—St. Matthew 11:28-30

But his call to the Gentile nations is going to end when that last person in God's number comes in.

> *"After this I beheld, and, lo, a great multitude, which no man could number, of all nations, and kindreds, and people, and tongues, stood before the throne, and before the Lamb, clothed with white robes, and palms in their hands;"*—Revelation 7:9

The day is coming when we can no longer be saved. Salvation will go back to the Jews.

> *"For I would not, brethren, that ye should be ignorant of this mystery, lest ye should be wise in your own conceits; that blindness in part is happened to Israel, until the fulness of the Gentiles be come in. And so all Israel shall be saved: as it is written, There shall come out of Zion the Deliverer, and shall turn away ungodliness from Jacob:"*—Romans 11:25-26

> *"And after these things I saw four angels standing on the four corners of the earth, holding the four winds of the earth, that the wind should not blow on the earth, nor on the sea, nor on any tree. And I saw another angel ascending from the east, having the seal of the living God: and he cried with a loud voice to the four angels, to whom it was given to hurt the earth and the sea, Saying,*

> *Hurt not the earth, neither the sea, nor the trees, till we have sealed the servants of our God in their foreheads. And I heard the number of them which were sealed: and there were sealed an hundred and forty and four thousand of all the tribes of the children of Israel. Of the tribe of Judah were sealed twelve thousand. Of the tribe of Reuben were sealed twelve thousand. Of the tribe of Gad were sealed twelve thousand. Of the tribe of Aser were sealed twelve thousand. Of the tribe of Nephthalim were sealed twelve thousand. Of the tribe of Manasses were sealed twelve thousand. Of the tribe of Simeon were sealed twelve thousand. Of the tribe of Levi were sealed twelve thousand. Of the tribe of Issachar were sealed twelve thousand. Of the tribe of Zabulon were sealed twelve thousand. Of the tribe of Joseph were sealed twelve thousand. Of the tribe of Benjamin were sealed twelve thousand"*—Revelation 7:1-8

The Gentile nations must come into Jesus before God takes in that last Gentile, leaving to them only the thousand year period for them to have peace before Satan is turned loose to deceive them again, and they will not pass the test.

> *"And when the thousand years are expired, Satan shall be loosed out of his prison,"*—Revelation 20:7

If you as a Gentile want to escape, you must be ready for the Rapture. You must **"be purified, and made white, and tried"**, but pass your test before the feet of the image of Nebuchadnezzar's dream comes in. For that is the Ten Toe Kingdom of Satan and his anti-Christ, which will be the man of the hour. He will be given authority over the world for that last week that consists of the last seven years of the seventy week period. It is that last week.

> *"Many shall be purified, and made white, and tried; but the wicked shall do wickedly: and none of the wicked shall understand; but the wise shall understand."*—Daniel 12:10

This seven year period of the Ten Toe Kingdom, whose leader is the anti-Christ and Satan is known as Jacob's trouble. It also speaks of a time when God will cause Israel and Judah to go into captivity, which they did until 1948 when God caused them to become a nation.

"The word that came to Jeremiah from the LORD, saying, Thus speaketh the LORD God of Israel, saying, Write thee all the words that I have spoken unto thee in a book. For, lo, the days come, saith the LORD, that I will bring again the captivity of my people Israel and Judah, saith the LORD: and I will cause them to return to the land that I gave to their fathers, and they shall possess it. And these are the words that the LORD spake concerning Israel and concerning Judah. For thus saith the LORD; We have heard a voice of trembling, of fear, and not of peace. Ask ye now, and see whether a man doth travail with child? wherefore do I see every man with his hands on his loins, as a woman in travail, and all faces are turned into paleness? Alas! for that day is great, so that none is like it: it is even the time of Jacob's trouble; but he shall be saved out of it. For it shall come to pass in that day, saith the LORD of hosts, that I will break his yoke from off thy neck, and will burst thy bonds, and strangers shall no more serve themselves of him: But they shall serve the LORD their God, and David their king, whom I will raise up unto them. Therefore fear thou not, O my servant Jacob, saith the LORD; neither be dismayed, O Israel: for, lo, I will save thee from afar, and thy seed from the land of their captivity; and Jacob shall return, and shall be in rest, and be quiet, and none shall make him afraid."—Jeremiah 30:1-10

The Ten Toe Kingdom will be broken to pieces by Jesus Christ's return.

"Thou sawest till that a stone was cut out without hands, which smote the image upon his feet that were of iron and clay, and brake them to pieces. Then was the iron, the clay, the brass, the silver, and the gold, broken to pieces together,

and became like the chaff of the summer threshingfloors; and the wind carried them away, that no place was found for them: and the stone that smote the image became a great mountain, and filled the whole earth. This is the dream; and we will tell the interpretation thereof before the king. Thou, O king, art a king of kings: for the God of heaven hath given thee a kingdom, power, and strength, and glory. And wheresoever the children of men dwell, the beasts of the field and the fowls of the heaven hath he given into thine hand, and hath made thee ruler over them all. Thou art this head of gold. And after thee shall arise another kingdom inferior to thee, and another third kingdom of brass, which shall bear rule over all the earth. And the fourth kingdom shall be strong as iron: forasmuch as iron breaketh in pieces and subdueth all things: and as iron that breaketh all these, shall it break in pieces and bruise. And whereas thou sawest the feet and toes, part of potters' clay, and part of iron, the kingdom shall be divided; but there shall be in it of the strength of the iron, forasmuch as thou sawest the iron mixed with miry clay. And as the toes of the feet were part of iron, and part of clay, so the kingdom shall be partly strong, and partly broken. And whereas thou sawest iron mixed with miry clay, they shall mingle themselves with the seed of men: but they shall not cleave one to another, even as iron is not mixed with clay. And in the days of these kings shall the God of heaven set up a kingdom, which shall never be destroyed: and the kingdom shall not be left to other people, but it shall break in pieces and consume all these kingdoms, and it shall stand for ever. Forasmuch as thou sawest that the stone was cut out of the mountain without hands, and that it brake in pieces the iron, the brass, the clay, the silver, and the gold; the great God hath made known to the king what shall come to pass hereafter: and the dream is certain, and the interpretation thereof sure."—Daniel 2:34-45

The Ten Toe Kingdom's end comes after seven years with the judgment of the living nations, and righteous government begins.

> *"For unto us a child is born, unto us a son is given: and the government shall be upon his shoulder: and his name shall be called Wonderful, Counsellor, The mighty God, The everlasting Father, The Prince of Peace. Of the increase of his government and peace there shall be no end, upon the throne of David, and upon his kingdom, to order it, and to establish it with judgment and with justice from henceforth even for ever. The zeal of the LORD of hosts will perform this."*—Isaiah 9:6-7

> *"And I saw heaven opened, and behold a white horse; and he that sat upon him was called Faithful and True, and in righteousness he doth judge and make war."*—Revelation 19:11

> *"When the Son of man shall come in his glory, and all the holy angels with him, then shall he sit upon the throne of his glory: And before him shall be gathered all nations: and he shall separate them one from another, as a shepherd divideth his sheep from the goats: And he shall set the sheep on his right hand, but the goats on the left. Then shall the King say unto them on his right hand, Come, ye blessed of my Father, inherit the kingdom prepared for you from the foundation of the world:"*—St. Matthew 25:31-34

This kingdom of righteous government is the Millennium Kingdom. This righteous kingdom lead by our Lord and Savior Jesus Christ will be one that lasts for one thousand years. It is a period when everyone will be treated right, and Satan will be locked up. At the end of it, Satan shall be let out of his prison.

> *"And I saw an angel come down from heaven, having the key of the bottomless pit and a great chain in his hand. And he laid hold on the dragon, that old serpent, which is the Devil, and Satan, and bound him a thousand years, And cast him into the bottomless pit, and shut him up, and set a seal upon him, that he should deceive the nations no more, till the thousand years should be fulfilled: and after that he must be loosed a little season. And I saw thrones,*

> *and they sat upon them, and judgment was given unto them: and I saw the souls of them that were beheaded for the witness of Jesus, and for the word of God, and which had not worshipped the beast, neither his image, neither had received his mark upon their foreheads, or in their hands; and they lived and reigned with Christ a thousand years. But the rest of the dead lived not again until the thousand years were finished. This is the first resurrection. Blessed and holy is he that hath part in the first resurrection: on such the second death hath no power, but they shall be priests of God and of Christ, and shall reign with him a thousand years. And when the thousand years are expired, Satan shall be loosed out of his prison, And shall go out to deceive the nations which are in the four quarters of the earth, Gog and Magog, to gather them together to battle: the number of whom is as the sand of the sea."*—Revelation 20:1-8

Satan will come back among the nations and cause them to be deceived again. He will cause the people of the world at that time to come against God one last time, and God will destroy them all together. It is at this time that God will judge. This judgment that will take place at the second resurrection, will take place at the Great White Throne judgment. It is the time of judgment for all that are not saved,

> *"And I saw a great white throne, and him that sat on it, from whose face the earth and the heaven fled away; and there was found no place for them. And I saw the dead, small and great, stand before God; and the books were opened: and another book was opened, which is the book of life: and the dead were judged out of those things which were written in the books, according to their works. And the sea gave up the dead which were in it; and death and hell delivered up the dead which were in them: and they were judged every man according to their works."*—Revelation 20:11-13

God's And Satan's Conversation About Job

In the beginning of the book of Job, it talks about a man that lived in the land of Uz, whose name was Job. It was said that this man was a "**perfect**" man.

> "There was a man in the land of Uz, whose name was Job; and that man was perfect and upright, and one that feared God, and eschewed evil. And there were born unto him seven sons and three daughters. His substance also was seven thousand sheep, and three thousand camels, and five hundred yoke of oxen, and five hundred she asses, and a very great household; so that this man was the greatest of all the men of the east. And his sons went and feasted in their houses, every one his day; and sent and called for their three sisters to eat and to drink with them. And it was so, when the days of their feasting were gone about, that Job sent and sanctified them, and rose up early in the morning, and offered burnt offerings according to the number of them all: for Job said, It may be that my sons have sinned, and cursed God in their hearts. Thus did Job continually. Now there was a day when the sons of God came to present themselves before the LORD, and Satan came also among them. And the LORD said unto Satan, Whence comest thou? Then Satan answered the LORD, and said, From going to and fro in the earth, and from

walking up and down in it. And the LORD said unto Satan, Hast thou considered my servant Job, that there is none like him in the earth, a perfect and an upright man, one that feareth God, and escheweth evil? Then Satan answered the LORD, and said, Doth Job fear God for nought? Hast not thou made an hedge about him, and about his house, and about all that he hath on every side? thou hast blessed the work of his hands, and his substance is increased in the land. But put forth thine hand now, and touch all that he hath, and he will curse thee to thy face. And the LORD said unto Satan, Behold, all that he hath is in thy power; only upon himself put not forth thine hand. So Satan went forth from the presence of the LORD."—Job 1:1-12

In the first chapter of Job, you will find a deep conversation going on between God and his ex-angel, Lucifer, who is now known as Satan. The conversation was about a man named Job. He was a man that hated evil. He had been blessed by God to have wealth that was greater than every man in the east. Job had children that did not want to live right. They would have feasts in all their houses because they loved to party.

"And his sons went and feasted in their houses, every one his day; and sent and called for their three sisters to eat and to drink with them. And it was so, when the days of their feasting were gone about, that Job sent and sanctified them, and rose up early in the morning, and offered burnt offerings according to the number of them all: for Job said, It may be that my sons have sinned, and cursed God in their hearts. Thus did Job continually."—Job 1:4-5

"While he was yet speaking, there came also another, and said, Thy sons and thy daughters were eating and drinking wine in their eldest brother's house: And, behold, there came a great wind from the wilderness, and smote the four corners of the house, and it fell upon the young men, and they are dead; and I only am escaped alone to tell thee."—Job 1:18-19

> *"The fool hath said in his heart, There is no God. They are corrupt, they have done abominable works, there is none that doeth good. The LORD looked down from heaven upon the children of men, to see if there were any that did understand, and seek God. They are all gone aside, they are all together become filthy: there is none that doeth good, no, not one. Have all the workers of iniquity no knowledge? who eat up my people as they eat bread, and call not upon the LORD."*—Psalm 14:1-4

Their father Job had a relationship with God, and he knew that his children were not being pleasing to his God. So when they would finish having these feasts, which had nothing to do with God, Job would send for them and sanctify them. He wanted them to be set apart as holy. He wanted God to purify them. He wanted them to be set free of their impurities, their pollutions. He would get up early in the morning and send up burnt offerings for them.

"Now there came a day when the <u>sons of God</u> came to present themselves before the Lord," Satan came amongst them. (Remember now, that these sons of God are not angels. We already covered that earlier.) When we as saints present ourselves in prayer and fasting, if there is anyway possible, Satan or his demons are going to come against us and try to cause us to break that fast.

God then asked Satan a question that proves to you and I that Satan will never be as smart as God. God said to him, "Whence comest thou?" Satan was so busy talking until he did not really hear or know what was going on.

> *"The way of a fool is right in his own eyes: but he that hearkeneth unto counsel is wise."*—Proverbs 12:15

God was setting Satan up to lose, and Job to win. He wanted Job to know Him like never before. He wanted Job to get a blessing like never before. He wanted Job to see something that one can only see when you go through something that looks like it has come to destroy you. But in order for him to get what God had for him, he had to learn how to suffer.

God asked Satan two questions, but like always, Satan thought that he was a match for God. He thought he had the power to pluck out of God's hand, a child of God. One that was before ordained to suffer this trying experience. God wanted Job to know Him better and also to know himself more favorably. Satan thought that he was a match for God, so much so until he missed out completely on what was going on.

> *"A brutish man knoweth not; neither doth a fool understand this."*—Psalm 92:6

God's conversation with him was over his head. When you get to a place in your intelligence, that you make yourself believe that you can outsmart God, there is something wrong. Don't ever become so foolish that you let something like that get into your psyche. **DON'T BECOME A FOOL!!**

What Satan did not catch, is that there is <u>no question mark in the Lord!!</u> If God asks you a question, He does not do it because He does not know where you are or what you are doing. God is omnipresent, He is everywhere. He is omniscient, He knows all things. Daniel said this.

> *"But there is a God in heaven that revealeth secrets, and maketh known to the king Nebuchadnezzar what shall be in the latter days. Thy dream, and the visions of thy head upon thy bed, are these;"*—Daniel 2:28

God knew where Satan was and what he was doing before the question was asked. When God asked that question, what Satan should have said was, "Sir, thou knowest."

Job found out that there was nothing too hard for God. At the end of his test, Job said these words.

> *"Then Job answered the LORD, and said, I know that thou canst do every thing, and that no thought can be withholden from thee. Who is he that hideth counsel without knowledge? therefore have I uttered that I understood not; things too wonderful for me, which I knew not. Hear, I beseech thee, and I will speak: I will demand of thee, and declare thou unto me. I have heard of thee by the hearing of the ear: but now mine eye seeth thee."*—Job 42:1-5

The Mystery Of The Olive Trees

This mystery of the olive trees deals with two olive trees. One is the natural tree, which represents the Jewish nation, Israel. The other is a wild olive tree which represents the Gentile nations.

"I say then, Hath God cast away his people? God forbid. For I also am an Israelite, of the seed of Abraham, of the tribe of Benjamin. God hath not cast away his people which he foreknew. Wot ye not what the scripture saith of Elias? how he maketh intercession to God against Israel, saying, Lord, they have killed thy prophets, and digged down thine altars; and I am left alone, and they seek my life. But what saith the answer of God unto him? I have reserved to myself seven thousand men, who have not bowed the knee to the image of Baal. Even so then at this present time also there is a remnant according to the election of grace. And if by grace, then is it no more of works: otherwise grace is no more grace. But if it be of works, then is it no more grace: otherwise work is no more work. What then? Israel hath not obtained that which he seeketh for; but the election hath obtained it, and the rest were blinded (According as it is written, God hath given them the spirit of slumber, eyes that they should not see, and ears that they should not hear;) unto this day. And David saith, Let their table be made a snare, and a trap, and a stumblingblock, and a recompence unto them: Let their eyes be darkened, that they may not see, and bow

down their back always. I say then, Have they stumbled that they should fall? God forbid: but rather through their fall salvation is come unto the Gentiles, for to provoke them to jealousy. Now if the fall of them be the riches of the world, and the diminishing of them the riches of the Gentiles; how much more their fulness? For I speak to you Gentiles, inasmuch as I am the apostle of the Gentiles, I magnify mine office: If by any means I may provoke to emulation them which are my flesh, and might save some of them. For if the casting away of them be the reconciling of the world, what shall the receiving of them be, but life from the dead? For if the firstfruit be holy, the lump is also holy: and if the root be holy, so are the branches. And if some of the branches be broken off, and thou, being a wild olive tree, wert grafted in among them, and with them partakest of the root and fatness of the olive tree; Boast not against the branches. But if thou boast, thou bearest not the root, but the root thee. Thou wilt say then, The branches were broken off, that I might be grafted in. Well; because of unbelief they were broken off, and thou standest by faith. Be not highminded, but fear: For if God spared not the natural branches, take heed lest he also spare not thee. Behold therefore the goodness and severity of God: on them which fell, severity; but toward thee, goodness, if thou continue in his goodness: otherwise thou also shalt be cut off. And they also, if they abide not still in unbelief, shall be grafted in: for God is able to graft them in again. For if thou wert cut out of the olive tree which is wild by nature, and wert grafted contrary to nature into a good olive tree: how much more shall these, which be the natural branches, be grafted into their own olive tree? For I would not, brethren, that ye should be ignorant of this mystery, lest ye should be wise in your own conceits; that blindness in part is happened to Israel, until the fulness of the Gentiles be come in."—Romans 11:1-25

Israel was a very disobedient people who longed for God, but when He came as a mighty man, they did not receive Him.

> *"He was in the world, and the world was made by him, and the world knew him not. He came unto his own, and his own received him not. But as many as received him, to them gave he power to become the sons of God, even to them that believe on his name: Which were born, not of blood, nor of the will of the flesh, nor of the will of man, but of God. And the Word was made flesh, and dwelt among us, (and we beheld his glory, the glory as of the only begotten of the Father,) full of grace and truth."*—St. John 1:10-14

They hated Jesus so much until they could not see what he was about. So because of their unbelief, they did not receive what God had sent to them. They felt like they were the only people God had. Since their attitude was like that, they did not obtain that which they were seeking. Therefore, God gave them over to the spirit of slumber. They were placed in an inactive state. They stumble over the name of Jesus, even until this day. But God has not forgotten His people. Because of Israel's fall, salvation came to us, the Gentiles. Paul told the Gentiles that he was their apostle and that if he could, he was going to "**provoke to emulation**" his people, Israel, to equal or surpass the Gentiles when it came to loving Jesus.

Paul was saying that "**if the casting away**" of his people were "**the reconciling of the world,**" they would be received again. The branches of the tree of God are holy. At one time, all the branches of this tree were Jews. There were no other branches. But when they rejected Jesus, most of their branches were broken off so that we, the Gentile race, could be grafted into God's olive tree, into the body of Christ. It was because of Israel's skepticism that they were broken off and we came in by faith. The Gentile branches (saints) from their wild olive tree (world) will continue to be grafted in, until the fullness (completion) of the Gentiles comes in (last Gentile in the number God has chosen to be a part of the body of Christ comes in).

> *"After this I beheld, and, lo, a great multitude, which no man could number, of all nations, and kindreds, and people, and tongues, stood before the throne, and before the Lamb, clothed with white robes, and palms in their hands; And cried with a loud voice, saying, Salvation to our God which sitteth upon the throne, and unto the Lamb. And all the angels stood round about the throne,*

and about the elders and the four beasts, and fell before the throne on their faces, and worshipped God, Saying, Amen: Blessing, and glory, and wisdom, and thanksgiving, and honour, and power, and might, be unto our God for ever and ever. Amen. And one of the elders answered, saying unto me, What are these which are arrayed in white robes? and whence came they? And I said unto him, Sir, thou knowest. And he said to me, These are they which came out of great tribulation, and have washed their robes, and made them white in the blood of the Lamb."—Revelation 7: 9-14

This tribulation period in verse 14 is not Jacob's trouble period which takes place during the Great Tribulation Period. This is the great troubles that we are going through today. These great troubles will go on until the fullness of the Gentiles comes in. Then the next seven years, the anti-Christ's reign, will be Jacob's trouble.

The Mystery Of The New Jerusalem

> *"Behold, I come quickly: hold that fast which thou hast, that no man take thy crown. Him that overcometh will I make a pillar in the temple of my God, and he shall go no more out: and I will write upon him the name of my God, and the name of the city of my God, which is new Jerusalem, which cometh down out of heaven from my God: and I will write upon him my new name. He that hath an ear, let him hear what the Spirit saith unto the churches."*—Revelation 3:11-13

I have heard many schools of thoughts about this city, the New Jerusalem. I have heard songs of how we are going to walk around in it. I have heard how beautiful the city is going to look, and that's all true. The city is beautiful. I have heard of buildings that are going to be there that are more excellent than these buildings on earth, made by man. In fact, the buildings we live in here on earth can not compare to the houses in the New Jerusalem. These homes are mansions that are in the New Jerusalem, and these mansions are in God.

> *"In my Father's house are many mansions: if it were not so, I would have told you. I go to prepare a place for you. And if I go and prepare a place for you, I will come again, and receive you unto myself; that where I am, there ye may be also. And whither I go ye know, and the way ye know,"*—St. John 14:2-4

Every part of the New Jerusalem is about the saints of God. In fact, the New Jerusalem and everything in it, is made up of the saints.

"And there came unto me one of the seven angels which had the seven vials full of the seven last plagues, and talked with me, saying, Come hither, I will <u>show thee</u> the bride, the <u>Lamb's wife.</u> And he carried me away in the spirit to a great and high mountain, and <u>showed</u> me that <u>great city, the holy Jerusalem</u>, descending out of heaven from God, Having the glory of God: and <u>her</u> light was like unto a stone most precious, even like a jasper stone, clear as crystal; And had a wall great and high, and had twelve gates, and at the gates twelve angels, and names written thereon, which are the names of the twelve tribes of the children of Israel: On the east three gates; on the north three gates; on the south three gates; and on the west three gates. And the wall of the city had twelve foundations, and in them the names of the twelve apostles of the Lamb. And he that talked with me had a golden reed to measure the city, and the gates thereof, and the wall thereof. And the city lieth foursquare, and the length is as large as the breadth: and he measured the city with the reed, twelve thousand furlongs. The length and the breadth and the height of it are equal. And he measured the wall thereof, an hundred and forty and four cubits, according to the measure of a man, that is, of the angel. And the building of the wall of it was of jasper: and the city was pure gold, like unto clear glass. And the foundations of the wall of the city were garnished with all manner of precious stones. The first foundation was jasper; the second, sapphire; the third, a chalcedony; the fourth, an emerald; The fifth, sardonyx; the sixth, sardius; the seventh, chrysolite; the eighth, beryl; the ninth, a topaz; the tenth, a chrysoprasus; the eleventh, a jacinth; the twelfth, an amethyst. And the twelve gates were twelve pearls;: every several gate was of one pearl: and the street of the city was pure gold, as it were transparent glass. And I saw no temple therein: for the Lord God Almighty and the Lamb are the temple of it. And the city had no need of the sun, neither of the moon,

> *to shine in it: for the glory of God did lighten it, and the Lamb is the light thereof. And the nations of them which are saved shall walk in the light of it: and the kings of the earth do bring their glory and honour into it. And the gates of it shall not be shut at all by day: for there shall be no night there. And they shall bring the glory and honour of the nations into it. And there shall in no wise enter into it any thing that defileth, neither whatsoever worketh abomination, or maketh a lie: but they which are written in the Lamb's book of life."*—Revelation 21:9-27

The angel that came and talked to John said, "**Come hither, I will <u>show thee</u> the <u>bride</u>** . . ." John said that "**he**" then "**carried me away in the spirit to a great and high mountain, and <u>showed</u> me that <u>great city</u>, the holy Jerusalem** . . ." Now John was looking to see the bride of the Lamb and he did see the bride. The bride and the holy Jerusalem (New Jerusalem) were one and the same. Every description of this city pertained to the saints of God. From the twelve gates, which represent the twelve tribes, to the twelve foundations which represent the twelve apostles that were started by the chief corner stone, **Jesus.**

> *"For through him we both have access by one Spirit unto the Father. Now therefore ye are no more strangers and foreigners, but fellowcitizens with the saints, and of the household of God; And are built upon the foundation of the apostles and prophets, Jesus Christ himself being the chief corner stone; In whom all the building fitly framed together groweth unto an holy temple in the Lord: In whom ye also are builded together for an habitation of God through the Spirit."*—Ephesians 2:18-22

> *"To whom coming, as unto a living stone, disallowed indeed of men, but chosen of God, and precious, Ye also, as lively stones, are built up a spiritual house, an holy priesthood, to offer up spiritual sacrifices, acceptable to God by Jesus Christ. Wherefore also it is contained in the scripture, Behold, I lay in Zion a chief corner stone, elect, precious: and he that believeth on him shall not be confounded."*—I Peter 2:4-6

We the saints of God are the New Jerusalem. The city is still being built and when the last living stone is in place and caught up to be with the Lord, the jewels in this city will all be in place and these jewels are the saints of God.

> *"Ye have said, It is vain to serve God: and what profit is it that we have kept his ordinance, and that we have walked mournfully before the LORD of hosts? And now we call the proud happy; yea, they that work wickedness are set up; yea, they that tempt God are even delivered. Then they that feared the LORD spake often one to another: and the LORD hearkened, and heard it, and a book of remembrance was written before him for them that feared the LORD, and that thought upon his name. And they shall be mine, saith the LORD of hosts, in that day when I make up my jewels; and I will spare them, as a man spareth his own son that serveth him. Then shall ye return, and discern between the righteous and the wicked, between him that serveth God and him that serveth him not."*—Malachi 3:14-18

Gold is what we become when going through our trials and tribulations.

> *"I counsel thee to buy of me gold tried in the fire, that thou mayest be rich; and white raiment, that thou mayest be clothed, and that the shame of thy nakedness do not appear; and anoint thine eyes with eyesalve, that thou mayest see."*—Revelation 3:18

> *"And I will bring the third part through the fire, and will refine them as silver is refined, and will try them as gold is tried: they shall call on my name, and I will hear them: I will say, It is my people: and they shall say, The LORD is my God."*—Zechariah 13:9

Everything about this city has something to do with the saints of God. This city has no sunlight shining upon it. The light of that city is Jesus Christ. And **"every knee shall bow, and every tongue shall confess**," that our Jesus is Lord Almighty. I can not wait to hear Him say, "**well done good and faithful servant, that he have been faithful over a few things. I will make thee ruler over many things: enter thou into the joy of thy Lord**" That is when we will receive a great reward.

The Mystery Of The Victory Over Death

This mystery of victory over death had been revealed to Apostle Paul that we gentiles might know what our life is all about. It is not just about this life, but it is also about the life to come. It is about you making a very important decision as where you are going to spend your everlasting life. Every person that comes into this world will wind up in one of two places, with Jesus in paradise as part of the New Jerusalem, or in the lake of fire, which most people know as hell.

> *"And the gates of it shall not be shut at all by day: for there shall be no night there. And they shall bring the glory and honour of the nations into it. And there shall in no wise enter into it any thing that defileth, neither whatsoever worketh abomination, or maketh a lie: but they which are written in the Lamb's book of life."*—Revelation 21:25-27

> *"And there shall be no more curse: but the throne of God and of the Lamb shall be in it; and his servants shall serve him: And they shall see his face; and his name shall be in their foreheads. And there shall be no night there; and they need no candle, neither light of the sun; for the Lord God giveth them light: and they shall reign for ever and ever. And he said unto me, These sayings are faithful and true: and the Lord God of the holy prophets sent his angel*

to show unto his servants the things which must shortly be done. Behold, I come quickly: blessed is he that keepeth the sayings of the prophecy of this book."—Revelation 22:3-7

The other place is not a nice place to go to.

And there was a certain beggar named Lazarus, which was laid at his gate, full of sores. And desiring to be fed with the crumbs which fell from the rich man's table: moreover the dogs came and licked his sores. And it came to pass, that the beggar died, and was carried by the angels into Abraham's bosom: the rich man also died, and was buried. And in hell he lift up his eyes, being in torments, and sooth Abraham afar off, and Lazarus in his bosom. And he cried and said, Father Abraham, have mercy on me, and send Lazarus, that he may dip the tip of his finger in water, and cool my tongue; for I am tormented in this flame. But Abraham said, Son, remember that thou in thy lifetime receivedst thy good things, and likewise Lazarus evil things: but now he is comforted, and thou art tormented. And beside all this, between us and you there is a great gulf fixed: so that they which would pass from hence to you cannot; neither can they pass to us, that would come from thence. Then he said, I pray thee therefore, father, that though wouldest send him to my father's house: For I have five brethren; that he may testify unto them, lest they also come into this place of torment. Abraham saith unto him, They have Moses and the prophets; let them hear them. And he said, Nay, father Abraham: but if one went unto them from the dead, they will repent. And he said unto him, If they hear not Moses and the prophets, neither will they be persuaded, though one rose the dead.—St. Luke 16: 20-31

The Son of man shall send forth his angels, and they shall gather out of his kingdom and all things that offend, and them which do "uniquity"; "And shall cast them into furnace of fire: "there shall be wailing and gnashing of teeth. "Then shall the righteous shine forth as the sun in the kingdom of their Father, "Who hath ears to hear, let them hear.—St. Matthew 13:41-43

"Wherefore if thy hand or thy foot offend thee, cut them off, and cast them from thee: it is better for thee to enter into life "halt" or "maimed", rather than having two hands or two feet to be cast into everlasting fire.— St. Matthew 18:8

"And the devil that deceived them was cast into the lake of fire and brimstone, where the beast and the false prophet are, and shall be tormented day and night for ever and ever."—Revelation 20:10

This place where they go to spend everlasting life is the lake of fire where Satan will enter into his second death along with everyone that is not in the New Jerusalem. The last one that will be cast into it, is death itself.

"Behold, I show you a mystery; We shall not all sleep, but we shall all be changed, In a moment, in the twinkling of an eye, at the last trump: for the trumpet shall sound, and the dead shall be raised incorruptible, and we shall be changed. For this corruptible must put on incorruption, and this mortal must put on immortality. So when this corruptible shall have put on incorruption, and this mortal shall have put on immortality, then shall be brought to pass the saying that is written, Death is swallowed up in victory. O death, where is thy sting? O grave, where is thy victory? The sting of death is sin; and the strength of sin is the law. But thanks be to God, which giveth us the victory through our Lord Jesus Christ. Therefore, my beloved brethren, be ye stedfast, unmoveable, always abounding in the work of the Lord, forasmuch as ye know that your labour is not in vain in the Lord."—I Corinthians 15:51-58

The only way one can avoid the second death that will keep you in everlasting limbo, in a life of neglect and oblivion for those who chose to live in sin all their lives, is to be raptured with the saints. Death can only sting you in the second death. The first death can not be compared to the second death. The first death is of the flesh, but the second death is of the soul and spirit, and it lasts forever. These people that go through the second death are found in the books. There are so many sinners until it is going to take more then one book to record their names.

> *"Enter ye in at the strait gate: for wide is the gate, and broad is the way, that leadeth to destruction, and many there be which go in thereat: Because strait is the gate, and narrow is the way, which leadeth unto life, and few there be that find it."*—St. Matthew 7:13-14

> *"And I saw a great white throne, and him that sat on it, from whose face the earth and the heaven fled away; and there was found no place for them. And I saw the dead, small and great, stand before God; and the books were opened: and another book was opened, which is the book of life: and the dead were judged out of those things which were written in the books, according to their works. And the sea gave up the dead which were in it; and death and hell delivered up the dead which were in them: and they were judged every man according to their works. And death and hell were cast into the lake of fire. This is the second death. And whosoever was not found written in the book of life was cast into the lake of fire."*—Revelation 20:11-15

The second death lead to the judgment of the sinners (or the dead).

Everyone that enters into this world in the flesh must die that first death, even if you enter and are translated to some other place as Enoch and Elijah. Even though they walked with God, they must experience the first death. These two Enoch and Elijah which are chosen by God for a special work, must return because they did not die. Therefore, these two must be the chosen two prophets that are to lead among the 144,000 Jews.

Even Melchizedek who was said to be **"a priest for ever"**, who had no mother or father, no beginning or no end, had to come back and die. This man was none other than Jesus.

> *"For it is evident that our Lord sprang out of Judah; of which tribe Moses spake nothing concerning priesthood. And it is yet far more evident: for that after the similitude of Melchisedec there ariseth another priest, Who is made, not after the law of a carnal commandment, but after the power of an endless life. For he testifieth, Thou art a priest for ever after the order of Melchisedec. For there is verily a disannulling of the commandment going before for the weakness and unprofitableness thereof. For the law made nothing perfect, but the bringing in of a better hope did; by the which we draw nigh unto God. And inasmuch as not without an oath he was made priest: (For those priests were made without an oath; but this with an oath by him that said unto him, The Lord sware and will not repent, Thou art a priest for ever after the order of Melchisedec:) By so much was Jesus made a surety of a better testament."*—Hebrews 7:14-22

Once a person dies, they await God's judgment. Those that die in Christ will come back with him and will be judge in the clouds. Those that are alive and remain when Jesus come **"will be caught up together with them to meet the Lord in the air."**

> *"But I would not have you to be ignorant, brethren, concerning them which are asleep, that ye sorrow not, even as others which have no hope. For if we believe that Jesus died and rose again, even so them also which sleep in Jesus will God bring with him. For this we say unto you by the word of the Lord, that we which are alive and remain unto the coming of the Lord shall not prevent them which are asleep. For the Lord himself shall descend from heaven with a shout, with the voice of the archangel, and with the trump of God: and the dead in Christ shall rise first: Then we which are alive and remain shall be caught up together with them in the clouds, to meet the Lord in the air: and so shall we ever be with the Lord. Wherefore comfort one another with these words"*—I Thessalonians 4:13-18

There are three parts to the first resurrection, which all partakers are raptured. The first part is "**Christ**," "**the first fruits of them that slept.**" The second part is those that are Christ's, whether dead or alive, when he comes to rapture the saints. (I Thessalonians 4:13-17) Their judgment is in the clouds for those that are written in the <u>BOOK.</u> The third part is when the last two prophets are killed by the anti-Christ and after three and a half days, they are called up to Heaven.

> *"And when they shall have finished their testimony, the beast that ascendeth out of the bottomless pit shall make war against them, and shall overcome them, and kill them. And their dead bodies shall lie in the street of the great city, which spiritually is called Sodom and Egypt, where also our Lord was crucified. And they of the people and kindreds and tongues and nations shall see their dead bodies three days and an half, and shall not suffer their dead bodies to be put in graves. And they that dwell upon the earth shall rejoice over them, and make merry, and shall send gifts one to another; because these two prophets tormented them that dwelt on the earth. And after three days and an half the spirit of life from God entered into them, and they stood upon their feet; and great fear fell upon them which saw them. And they heard a great voice from heaven saying unto them, Come up hither. And they ascended up to heaven in a cloud; and their enemies beheld them."*—Revelation 11:7-12

But in the judgment of the living dead, this is what happens.

> *"And I saw a great white throne, and him that sat on it, from whose face the earth and the heaven fled away; and there was found no place for them. And I saw the dead, small and great, stand before God; and the books were opened: and another book was opened, which is the book of life: and the dead were judged out of those things which were written in the books, according to their works. And the sea gave up the dead which were in it; and death and hell delivered up the dead which were in them: and they were judged every man according to their works. And*

death and hell were cast into the lake of fire. This is the second death. And whosoever was not found written in the book of life was cast into the lake of fire."—Revelation 20:11-15

After this, there are no more that are found in the book of life, only those who are saved according to the word of God. It is being taught that there will be people saved in the Millennium Kingdom, but that is not true. It is a lie from the pit of Hell to make Gentiles believe that they have another chance to be saved after the Rapture.

The last person that goes into the lake of fire is death.

"And there shall in no wise enter into it any thing that defileth, neither whatsoever worketh abomination, or maketh a lie: but they which are written in the Lamb's book of life."—Revelation 21:27

"For I testify unto every man that heareth the words of the prophecy of this book, If any man shall add unto these things, God shall add unto him the plagues that are written in this book: And if any man shall take away from the words of the book of this prophecy, God shall take away his part out of the book of life, and out of the holy city, and from the things which are written in this book. He which testifieth these things saith, Surely I come quickly. Amen. Even so, come, Lord Jesus. The grace of our Lord Jesus Christ be with you all. Amen."—Revelation 22:18-21

"Behold, I shew you a mystery; We shall not all sleep, but we shall all be changed, `In a moment, in the twinkling of an eye, at the last trump: for the trumpet shall sound, and the dead shall be raised incorruptible, and we shall be changed. For this corruptible must put on incorruption, and this mortal must put on immortality. So when this corruptible shall have put on incorruption, and this mortal shall have put on immortality, then shall be brought to pass the saying that is written, Death is swallowed up in victory. O death, where is thy sting? O grave, where is thy victory"—I Corinthians 15:51-55

I call this death a "twinkling of an eye death" because the flesh must return to the dust. We are not all coming from the grave. Some of us will be alive when he comes. This body will and must die because it can not enter into the kingdom of God.

> *"Now this I say, brethren, that flesh and blood cannot inherit the kingdom of God; neither doth corruption inherit incorruption."*—I Corinthians 15:50

At the great white throne, when the judgment takes place, all those that die in sin's bodies, must be set free, whether their graves are in the sea or in earth.

> *"And I saw a great white throne, and him that sat on it, from whose face the earth and the heaven fled away; and there was found no place for them. And I saw the dead, small and great, stand before God; and the books were opened: and another book was opened, which is the book of life: and the dead were judged out of those things which were written in the books, according to their works. And the sea gave up the dead which were in it; and death and hell delivered up the dead which were in them: and they were judged every man according to their works. And death and hell were cast into the lake of fire. This is the second death. And whosoever was not found written in the book of life was cast into the lake of fire."*—Revelation 20: 11-15

After Satan is cast into the lake of fire, then comes death turn because he is not needed anymore.

> *"The last enemy that shall be destroyed is death"*—I Corinthians 15:26

> *"And I will give power unto my two witnesses, and they shall prophesy a thousand two hundred and threescore days, clothed in sackcloth. These are the two olive trees, and the two candlesticks standing before the God of the earth. And if any man will hurt them, fire proceedeth out*

of their mouth, and devoureth their enemies: and if any man will hurt them, he must in this manner be killed. These have power to shut heaven, that it rain not in the days of their prophecy: and have power over waters to turn them to blood, and to smite the earth with all plagues, as often as they will. And when they shall have finished their testimony, the beast that ascendeth out of the bottomless pit shall make war against them, and shall overcome them, and kill them. And their dead bodies shall lie in the street of the great city, which spiritually is called Sodom and Egypt, where also our Lord was crucified. And they of the people and kindreds and tongues and nations shall see their dead bodies three days and an half, and shall not suffer their dead bodies to be put in graves. And they that dwell upon the earth shall rejoice over them, and make merry, and shall send gifts one to another; because these two prophets tormented them that dwelt on the earth. And after three days and an half the spirit of life from God entered into them, and they stood upon their feet; and great fear fell upon them which saw them. And they heard a great voice from heaven saying unto them, Come up hither. And they ascended up to heaven in a cloud; and their enemies beheld them."—Revelation 11:3-12

These two witnesses that are spoken of in this passage of scripture, have caused many debates. There are two schools of thought. One school of thought is that it is Moses and Elijah, the other is that it is Elijah and Enoch. Moses is the choice of some because of the following scriptures.

"And after six days Jesus taketh Peter, James, and John his brother, and bringeth them up into an high mountain apart, And was transfigured before them: and his face did shine as the sun, and his raiment was white as the light. And, behold, there appeared unto them Moses and Elias talking with him. Then answered Peter, and said unto Jesus, Lord, it is good for us to be here: if thou wilt, let us make here three tabernacles; one for thee, and one for Moses, and one for Elias. While he yet spake, behold, a bright cloud overshadowed them: and behold a voice out of the cloud, which said, This is my

beloved Son, in whom I am well pleased; hear ye him. And when the disciples heard it, they fell on their face, and were sore afraid. And Jesus came and touched them, and said, Arise, and be not afraid. And when they had lifted up their eyes, they saw no man, save Jesus only. And as they came down from the mountain, Jesus charged them, saying, Tell the vision to no man, until the Son of man be risen again from the dead. And his disciples asked him, saying, Why then say the scribes that Elias must first come? And Jesus answered and said unto them, Elias truly shall first come, and restore all things. But I say unto you, That Elias is come already, and they knew him not, but have done unto him whatsoever they listed. Likewise shall also the Son of man suffer of them."—St. Matthew 17:1-12

Moses was chosen by many because he was seen with Elias (Elijah) when Jesus was transfigured, and because Moses was the one that turned water into blood. But if you note the disciples, after seeing what they did, only asked about Elias coming back. Why not ask was Moses coming with him? I believe that it is Elijah and Enoch. The reason why I believe that these two witnesses will be a part of the 144,000 saints that will be sealed by God in the Great Tribulation Period, and also chosen to lead them is this. I believe that Moses was representing Israel, the Old Testament, Jesus, the New Testament, the son of God, and Elijah, the 144,000 Jews. Although Moses performed that act of turning water into blood, one must remember that Moses was not the one that was doing this. He was only being used by God. Moses does not hold a patent on Gods' work, and besides, Moses died.

"Yet Michael the archangel, when contending with the devil he disputed about the body of Moses, durst not bring against him a railing accusation, but said, The Lord rebuke thee"—Jude 1:9

"Now after the death of Moses the servant of the LORD it came to pass, that the LORD spake unto Joshua the son of Nun, Moses' minister, saying, Moses my servant is dead; now therefore arise, go over this Jordan, thou, and all this people, unto the land which I do give to them, even to the children of Israel."—Joshua 1:1-2

Elijah and Elisha performed the same act of God.

> *"And fifty men of the sons of the prophets went, and stood to view afar off: and they two stood by Jordan. And Elijah took his mantle, and wrapped it together, and smote the waters, and they were divided hither and thither, so that they two went over on dry ground. And it came to pass, when they were gone over, that Elijah said unto Elisha, Ask what I shall do for thee, before I be taken away from thee. And Elisha said, I pray thee, let a double portion of thy spirit be upon me. And he said, Thou hast asked a hard thing: nevertheless, if thou see me when I am taken from thee, it shall be so unto thee; but if not, it shall not be so. And it came to pass, as they still went on, and talked, that, behold, there appeared a chariot of fire, and horses of fire, and parted them both asunder; and Elijah went up by a whirlwind into heaven. And Elisha saw it, and he cried, My father, my father, the chariot of Israel, and the horsemen thereof. And he saw him no more: and he took hold of his own clothes, and rent them in two pieces. He took up also the mantle of Elijah that fell from him, and went back, and stood by the bank of Jordan; And he took the mantle of Elijah that fell from him, and smote the waters, and said, Where is the LORD God of Elijah? and when he also had smitten the waters, they parted hither and thither: and Elisha went over."*—II Kings 2:7-14

There are only two men that were taking out of this world that have not died as of yet, and they are Elijah and Enoch. Both of them must come back to die so that the scripture may be fulfilled that is written in the word of God.

> *"And as it is appointed unto men once to die, but after this the judgment:"*—Hebrews 9:27

Even Jesus had to come back and die, because God's word has **gone forth and it can not come back void.**

> *"For as the rain cometh down, and the snow from heaven, and returneth not thither, but watereth the earth, and*

> *maketh it bring forth and bud, that it may give seed to the sower, and bread to the eater: So shall my word be that goeth forth out of my mouth: it shall not return unto me void, but it shall accomplish that which I please, and it shall prosper in the thing whereto I sent it."*—Isaiah 55:10-11

Death started with mankind in the creation of the world as we know it in Genesis with Adam and Eve.

> *"For as in Adam all die, even so in Christ shall all be made alive. But every man in his own order: Christ the firstfruits; afterward they that are Christ's at his coming. Then cometh the end, when he shall have delivered up the kingdom to God, even the Father; when he shall have put down all rule and all authority and power. For he must reign, till he hath put all enemies under his feet. The last enemy that shall be destroyed is death."*—I Corinthians 15:22-26

If Moses is the witness, what happens to Enoch? He left here alive and in his body, why was he taken? In order for this scripture to be fulfilled, he must come back and die before the judgment of the saints is complete. He can not enter into the kingdom of God with flesh and blood. Just as God has a reason and purpose for taking a Elijah from one period of time to another, so he had a reason and purpose for removing Enoch. Melchisedec came as a man, and even he had to come back as the man Jesus and die. He has no mother and father, no beginning and no end, but he was in the flesh. Jesus has a beginning,

> *"In whom we have redemption through his blood, even the forgiveness of sins: Who is the image of the invisible God, the firstborn of every creature:"*—Colossians 1:14-15

and he had an end.

> *"I am he that liveth, and was dead; and, behold, I am alive for evermore, Amen; and have the keys of hell and of death."*—Revelation 1:18

And yet, he has no beginning and he has no end, no mother and no father.

> *"In the beginning was the Word, and the Word was with God, and the Word was God. The same was in the beginning with God. All things were made by him; and without him was not any thing made that was made."*—St John 1:1-3

> *"Behold, he cometh with clouds; and every eye shall see him, and they also which pierced him: and all kindreds of the earth shall wail because of him. Even so, Amen. I am Alpha and Omega, the beginning and the ending, saith the Lord, which is, and which was, and which is to come, the Almighty"*—Revelation 1:7-8

> *"And when I saw him, I fell at his feet as dead. And he laid his right hand upon me, saying unto me, Fear not; I am the first and the last:"*—Revelation 1:17

Melchisedec and Jesus are one in the same.

> *"And Melchizedek king of Salem brought forth bread and wine: and he was the priest of the most high God."*—Genesis 14:18

> *"So also Christ glorified not himself to be made an high priest; but he that said unto him, Thou art my Son, to day have I begotten thee. As he saith also in another place, Thou art a priest for ever after the order of Melchisedec. Who in the days of his flesh, when he had offered up prayers and supplications with strong crying and tears unto him that was able to save him from death, and was heard in that he feared; Though he were a Son, yet learned he obedience by the things which he suffered; And being made perfect, he became the author of eternal salvation unto all them that obey him; Called of God an high priest after the order of Melchisedec"*—Hebrews 5:5-10

> *"For this Melchisedec, king of Salem, priest of the most high God, who met Abraham returning from the slaughter of the kings, and blessed him; To whom also Abraham gave a tenth part of all; first being by interpretation King of righteousness, and after that also King of Salem, which is, King of peace; Without father, without mother, without descent, having neither beginning of days, nor end of life; but made like unto the Son of God; abideth a priest continually."* —Hebrews 7:1-3

Both were in the flesh and as we know, Jesus came back to fulfill this scripture.

> *"And as it is appointed unto men once to die, but after this the judgment:"* —Hebrews 9:27

But most of all, he came back that we could be set free from darkness.

> *"I am he that liveth, and was dead; and, behold, I am alive for evermore, Amen; and have the keys of hell and of death."* —Revelation 1:18

Thanks be to God who gave us the victory.

To God be the Glory!!!!!

Prayer

Lord in the name of your son Jesus,

I pray that all that read this book receive the knowledge and wisdom therein. I ask that you reveal to all men and women of God your infinite wisdom. Let them see and teach your word to all the world, that someone will have ears to hear, to understand and to come out of darkness into your marvelous light. That your word be established in the minds of all men and women. I pray that you will continue to give man the mind to continue to read line upon line, line upon line, here a little, and there a litter, that they will not fall backwards and be broken. But that they come to the knowledge and the understanding of your word.

Thank you for using mankind to bring forth your truths. I will always praise your Holy Name, and give you the glory.

In Jesus name I pray, Amen.

If you were blessed by this book, I would like to hear from you! Feel free to write me at:

Pastor Ulysses L. Norris
1117 Westminister
Detroit, MI. 48211

WHOM SAY YE THAT I AM?